AMERICANS BY TURNS

Also by Chuck O'Neil

The Perfect Scar
Eating Out
Beyond Basilicas
Holding Things Together
better gods

SAWKILL FALLS EDITIONS

The Falls of the Sawkill
19th Century
Artist: Signature Illegible

for Celeste
for Ben, Chuck, Beth, Sarah

AMERICANS BY TURNS

Chuck O'Neil

CONTENTS

AMERICANS BY TURNS

*... Hope, then, to belong to your place
by your own knowledge of what it is
that no other place is, and by caring for
it as you care for no other place.*

— Wendell Berry
from 'A Poem on Hope'

Americans By Turns

for citizens to come
on our nation's 250th anniversary

1

We were the new blood once

And this place

Was the world of our days

Like you in your century

We cared for the things

That those who came before us

Left when they left

Parks   buildings   businesses

Monuments   markers   signs   street trees

An old bluestone fountain

Hill-woods   the glen

The creeks   the river

Ordinances   public hearings

Meeting minutes   codes   budgets

Word by written word

And word of mouth

A museum   food pantry   library   the VFW

Newspapers   lights   crosswalks   curb-cuts

Fields   bridges   intersections

Ambulance-fire-police
Snow removal   trash collection
Yes   all of it down to us

And we took care
Knowing our inheritance
Was in truth
Borrowed from our children
And held by us a while
In trust
For safekeeping

2
And we lived
Within shouting distance
Of each other
And from time to time
We shouted

Some swore
God was in the details
Some swore
It was the devil
Others were pretty sure
Details were just details

Yet we stood together for the flag
And said liberty and justice for all
And meant what we said

Because the town was ours then
And we were the town's
And day-in   day-out
The town to us was the county
The commonwealth   the country even
A nation of-by-and-for the people we could see
A republic we could keep

Where hope was local
And hope was the measure
Of everything held together
In trust
For safekeeping

3
And we learned early on
From our mothers and fathers
That we were born for hope
And seen by others everywhere
As the world's best hope

And hope was the thing with feathers
And hope begets hope
And a little of it
Goes a long way around the block
From house to house to house

And they taught us too
That hope is never a given
That   before you know it
Hope could be lost   or stolen
And warned us again and again
About the perils of indifference

And made certain we knew
There'd be times we'd need
To hope against hope
And that the cost for hope   like freedom
Is attention   vigilance always

Because it's hard to predict
The day or the hour
When the thief will come
And because the thief is clever
And oftentimes hides in plain sight

So we were watchful
Though prone to distraction
Attached to our comforts
Inclined to judge others
Impelled to be right

But the makers of our nation
Who saw firsthand
We could be our own worst enemies
Had faith-enough still
To look past daily human failings
To the better angels of our nature

As we look out now to you
New blood of the Union
Life by life by life
Imagining whatever was ours
Has become yours

And your history of flaws
And your hunger for hope
Not much different from ours

Citizens in your own time
Who are more to us
And more in our meditations
Than you might suppose

Taking care
Word by written word
And word of mouth
Reverencing a town's
Old bluestone fountain

Americans by turns
Keeping the republic
Holding up hope

Lines for The Knob

We see into the life of things
                    — Wordsworth
from 'Lines Composed Miles Above
Tintern Abbey'

Morning   noon   and in moonlight
   before the cities and the cemeteries
Before the demons and the hymns
   and the holy names

Before the first fires
   before paintings in caves
You stood in the mist
   under sun   thunder   snow

You whom the maker of mountains made
   whom we climb
To get a better picture
   of where we live

Watch over us
   in the village below
Busy always   earning our keep
   making the most of our days

And know
  there are times in town
From the yard
  the restaurant porch

Driving down Broad Street
  a second floor window
The post office parking lot
  when you come into view

A sight for our sore eyes
  your risen ground
Crowned with trees

Lodestar there
  at any hour   in every weather
Just as you are

Something for us to look up to

Through Glass Darkly

Winter through the window
A crescent moon halfway up
And the first tinge of orange
Beyond those hills

Snow in the yards
Roads still slick
And nobody out yet   except
The woman from around the corner
Heavy coat   scarf   boots   gloves   hat

Finding her footing beneath the streetlight
With the sizable gray-and-white dog
She fell heir to
When her daughter died

You watch   no   witness
You witness them
Leaving the glow
Leashed to each other   headed home
With the dog in the lead

And you can't help wishing

Our losses could be

Less set in stone

And heaven's ways

More like our own

Sweeney Adrift

Sweeney gave up smoking
    around the same time
He gave up drinking
    around the same time
He gave up going to church

Since   to his way of thinking
    it was pretty much church
(Up to its eyeballs in denials
    with god off in some other universe)
That drove him to smoke
    and drink in the first place

No doubt church
    had a ton to do
With the way a day would go
    from bad to worse
From left in the lurch
    to downright cursed in nothing flat

Like that time after work
    nearly dark   snow choking the roads
When his pickup snagged in a drift

And he leaps out
    swearing and swinging a shovel

Yelling about two-wheel drive
    beating dents and dings all down the side
Mirror busted off   taillight smashed in
    by the time he's done with the thing

I was sick to death after that
    for a good week or so   he says
Like I was ghosted by the angels

And me
    lapsed as I was by then
And no longer haunting the pews

Yeah   attack your own truck
    and brother   you know you got stuff
Way beyond snow to plow through

Not to make excuses
    but they say I was born
With my fists up
    and no god's gift right from the get-go

Hey you absolutely do
    what you need to do
To make ends meet
    gut it out   fight like the devil

And to tell you the truth
stuck as I was
Up to my elbows in snow
hell   I'm not so sure Christ Himself
Wouldn't've taken a few whacks
whaling on it like there's no tomorrow

Winging It

Standing in sand
Without Whitman
Wordsworth   Blake
A day of days for sure

And free to make what <u>you</u> make
Of this shoreful of beach birds
Blown down from the north

Scuttling on stubby stick legs
Their tan feathers shivering
As they zigzag silver stretches
Where waves've slid back

Following (more or less)
A wobbly lead bird
Who pecks there   there   there
And appears to be
Making it up as he goes

Yeah   time away
With no one here
To say one way or another

In the clear
And placing faith
In salt air   coastal light

And the whole flock
All-of-a-sudden taking flight

Winging it now
For those inlets
And mudflats to the south

from **Holding Things Together**

First Names

John Biddis 1749-1820

That summer   in August
    my settlement
By then a good-sized port
    was stricken with the fever

Death swept house-to-house
    like fire in a stiff wind
Yet   unlike so many others
    I was able to remove myself

My wife   my small children
    to lands I'd been told about
Up the river
    a fair distance to the north

Good air   rushing water
    hills rife with timber
A fine benchland there   the entirety of which
    I acquired before long

And built our cottage
    a mill   later a village
Laid out like my native city
    with straight alleys and straight streets

The son of immigrants
   I named this place   this outpost
For a town across the ocean
   where my ancestors lived

And   that their names might remain
   we christened certain of the east-west streets
After our sons and daughters   Anne   Catharine
   George   John   Sarah   Elizabeth

The Borough

I came to a village
Above a river
Hills all around it

The streets   wide by any measure
Were woven with alleys
Verged with trees in full leaf

And with architecture
Seldom seen standing together
In such a small town

And though I'd never
Passed those buildings before
I remembered them

And it seemed to me
I was always
From that place

I arrive today
As I arrived
Years ago

And recognize
Earlier villagers
As my kin

Their doorways before me
Rafters above me
Joists below me

Risers and treads to lift me
Railings they held once
To steady my step

I arrive by way of mortises and tenons
They've sawn and bit-braced
And fitted and pegged

All the handwork
Living in the buildings
Holding things together

Streetscape

Through the window
A work on paper

Charcoal by a local artist
An eye for streets
Before snow

The same grain and gray
Found in Historical Society prints
Hereabouts years ago

Unpaved in those days
And the yard across the way
Fenced waist-high
With ornamental iron

Maples   leafless   in rows
Already the borough appears
Lived-in many lifetimes

A similar linework now
Though the ancestor's
Fence is gone

Though that corner building
With the second story porch
(An inn   the caption says)
Went up in flames

The same names for streets
The same daylong dusk

And sycamores
Wintering out there
Standing for those
Early hand-drawn maples

Looking Out

for Tom Hoff   for Dick Snyder

It's a question of seeing
So much clearer

Of doing to things
What light does to them
            Guillevic
            Translation by Denise Levertov

Mid-November   late July

Who can say

How it is

Looking out a window

Drawn there by the light

Long slant of it

Across the wide street

Painter's light

The way   with shadow

Light sheds light

Over bluestone and brick

Over casings   plinths   quoins

As it blackens the glass

And steeps the brackets

Beneath the eaves in shade

And some nights
Who can say
How it was
With moonlight
By these entrances
These same sash

For souls who came before
Held for a time
Between the lintels and the sills

Wondering what to make
Of such glow
Of the way light migrates
Over all that was
Lifted into place
Lived in
And handed down

And how is it now
That those who are gone
Who it seems
Were just here
Are in town yet

Shedding light still
Long slant of it
Across the clapboard

Angling the alley   the walkway
The bench   the bollard   the verge
The planter   streetlamp   sign

Long light
Bridging the buildings
Sweeping the trees

Liberty Hill

We took down trees
That threatened the house

Smoothed off the bluff
From which they pitched

And opened it up
To sunlight

Bluebirds
The ridge across the river

We wore a path in time
Along our new verge

And sat in our bodies
And looked out in time from this rock

Innisfree   our little bit of it   anyway
This hilly reach above the streets

Spirit of it   the flowered rise
That rose within us

The Corner

> *. . . nothing is truly mine*
> *except my name. I only*
> *borrowed this dust.*
> Stanley Kunitz
> from *Passing Through*

1. Postcard *late 1800s*

We see you
There on the corner
In an earlier century

The newly-built courthouse
The old stone jail
Behind you

Not long
After our national war
Not so long
Before the World War

Fall
By the look of the trees
Afternoon
By the spill of the shadows

And light enough still
For the postcard photographer

Who's stood his camera
In the dirt middle of High Street
Lens leveled to the west
Vanishing point in the hill
At the end of the road
Rutted then   empty at that hour

Except for
The good-sized wagon
Hitched to the curb   (yours?)

And except   by luck   for you
Standing like any one of us
Hands in your coat
Staring down the years

2. Monument *1931*

We see so many of you
Gathered on the corner
To dedicate the monument
For soldiers and sailors

Fourth of July after a light rain
The courthouse
The old stone jail
Behind you

Not long
After the World War
And not so long
(Though you couldn't have known it)
Before the next one

Among you there   the Governor
A local man   man of his time
Mustached   rail-thin   statesmanlike
Hands by his side while speaking
From the bluestone top step
Of the ones who served
Of his hope for peace
From now on

And afterwards   smiling
In the photo with August Kiel
'The Marble King'   fellow townsman
Whose idea the memorial was
Who made a gift of it to the County

The benediction pronounced
By Reverend Arob
Taps played
By Louise Mulvaney
('star trumpeter'   'a slip of a girl')
Three veterans of the World War
Allen Meyers   Lee Thursby   Clarence McIlveen

Fire the salute
And the east corner of Centre Square
Becomes remembering ground

3. Today

We stand now
Where you stood
With the weather as it is
The courthouse
And the old stone jail
Behind us   as behind you then

Not so long
After Korea   Vietnam   The Gulf
While war goes on
In Afghanistan and the Middle East
And possibly not long
Before a flare-up somewhere else

Flags lowered
The wreath placed
Heads uncovered

We recognize
The town around us
Its hills   streams   river

And each of us

A dwelling place

For the Missing   the Unknowns

The ones who came home

We see ourselves

Keepers in our time

Of this corner

These names

Memorial Day, 2017
Milford, Pennsylvania

Plans and Elevations

Bless the house
A cottage really
Low ceilings   moonstruck windows
Pale hill rising behind it

And all the houses

And the full names
Of those who winter in them tonight
And the wintering ones before
And the ones still to come

Bless the porches
Dormers   gable ends
And let grief drift past the railings
And suffering lift away like smoke

Praise the plans and elevations
That outlast
That stand here
In the middle of a week
At the end of a year
Above ground
Open to the weather

River Road

for Paul McNeil

All finite things reveal their infinitude
Roethke

You saw early on
How the road begins
North of us

Where the river begins
Where water from the lake
Tumbles together
With water from the hills

And how one road
Threads the interior
And winds down
Along our drop-offs   rapids   wide pools

And levels up with the falls
And the sometimes-flooded fields
And scrolls through the oaks
And switchbacks as it rises above the ledges

From the overlook
Good Friend   the rain gone
May you see the whole of it

The town clear across the valley
The sun's rose streamers in the west

35

And may you see
The way you came
And the way now
Beside the river
Your road runs on

from **better gods**

Touchstone

for Eamon Grennan

Rescued from the utility crew's heap
When trenching pipe
Through Gooseberry Alley

We stood it in our yard
Beneath the trees
Where the driveway meets the street

And called the cemetery carver
To grave it about belt high
With our house number

Lion-colored among the evergreens
I pull weeds from the mulch
Around its base this morning

In the sway of sun and shade
Place my hand on its cool
Rain-clean skull

Old boulder   up from local clay

Laying groundwork

Reminding me

Miserere

for Jim Haggarty

Here   above town
Walls weave among the trees

Some look like
Rocks tossed together
To get them out of the way

Others   stacked from both sides
One-on-two   two-on-one
Stand as fencing still

And where the hill plateaus
A field long ago

Its view of the valley
Overrun with ramble rose
Clumped with saplings
Shagbark   a few red cedar

Heaven help those
Who are called away

Who leave their labor
When the time comes

Blessed are they who hay the high acres
And keep them clear for years and years

Maker of all days   incline your ear
And according to your mercy

Raise the ones who lift
So many stones

Closing

The realtor calls
To shift the closing
On account of the buyers' interpreter

Who works at a seafood place on The Sound
Open everyday but Thursday
Oh   and he's the owner
And the lone employee

So that last Thursday in May   sun just up
We get on the highway
And arrive mid-morning
A couple blocks from City Hall

All of us with ballpoints
Around a brown table
While the attorney circulates
Documents for signatures
Explains in plain English
As the interpreter deciphers
And the buyers nod

Soon   abruptly almost

Chairs roll back
And that was that

I (being the oldest)
Go over to the new owners
Say I believe our parents are happy
Their home sold to folks
Who worked so hard   saved so long

I wish them the best
And when the translator finishes
They nod   smile slightly

In the parking lot
We   the late living evidence
Of our mother and father   talk
Tear up   as after a wake

And we carry that ache to our cars
And wave
And drive off separate ways

Snow Day

Two girls at Ann Street Park
One in a light green jacket   with a shovel

The other in a red sweatshirt
That says *Lady Eagles*   with a ball

They clear part of the court
And talk and take shots

After a while
The sun breaks through
And the maples rain melting snow

And a few blocks over
A woman plans to leave
The one who swore to god
He wouldn't do it again

Now the girls make their way
Up Fifth Street
Turn left on Catharine
Talking the whole time
Middle-schoolers
Somebody's daughters

Cheering

It's a Saturday game
Parents lean against the link fence
Stand in the bleachers

A young dad barks nonstop
And the umpire   a volunteer fireman   I think
Seems to sweat every call

I consider going over to the dad
When the inning ends to say
I remember when an ump ruled
My son's first home run a double
And I yelled till he tossed me out

Or kid him
About a support group
For parents of Little Leaguers
With catchy topics like

Deep Breathing Between Innings
The Yelling Cessation Workshop
Bogus Calls and Authority Issues
When the F-Word Slips Out
Losing and the Ice Cream After

But I can see he's wound too tightly
For laughs just now

The truth is
I see him   and see myself
Knowing so little as a dad
Trying like hell
To cover all the bases

My yelling wasn't
As hereditary as I'd once imagined
(Though the Irish *are* a mouthy bunch)

Give him time
He'll figure things out

So I say
I can't believe my grown sons
Were once this small
And leave it at that

Last Roof

I meet with the roofer
On an Indian summer Friday
To upgrade our worn three-tabs
With something more 'architectural'

The look of a roof is key   he agrees
Here's one style
Perfect for a house in town

I'm drawn to the slate-like
Color   thickness   feel
And ask about warranty and price

He eyes me up and down   says
You'll be in the ground
Long before you even think about
Replacing these shingles
Definitely your last roof

I want it nice   I say
But hey   it's not the Vatican

I got these   he says (eyeing me sideways)
Won't set you back so bad
But depending on how things go
You <u>could</u> be lookin' at replacement
Maybe   maybe not

Can I take both samples home
To talk things over with my wife

No problem
Have 'em for the weekend   he says
Gimme a shout on Mondee
Tuesdee's ok too
So we get ya done
Before snow flies

Yup   Lord Willing
Before snow flies   I say   shutting the trunk
And   leaving well enough alone
Hold off asking
If he knows any good gutter guys

God's Acre

Remembrance Place Park
Milford, Pennsylvania

Perhaps in this neglected spot is laid
Some heart once pregnant with celestial fire . . .

from Elegy Written in a Country Churchyard
Thomas Gray 1751

1

So many unknowns
Above and below us

This park   a lost lot once
A graveyard for families
Going back lifetimes
With names we say today

For years   a neglected spot
Its mostly-marble headstones
Toppled   taken   flipped
Face down for walkways even

Or carted to the cemetery on the hill
Along with remains unearthed here
And reburied up there

Yet   remains remain still
Lord knows where

2

And lord knows
How they lived through those winters
When the river froze so thick
They could sled a house across it
From one state to the other

Lord knows
The hopes they clung to
Father   mother   worried sick
Over a newborn's cough and high fever
Mourning all the while their earlier loss

That arched stone in the grass
Half the average height and width
The word 'BABY' cut into it

3

Praise for this garden
And for its gardeners

And for what flowers   shrubs   and trees
Say about devotion

And for what these worn stones
Say about a small town

The way it goes on
Ending and beginning again

And bless those
Who remember to remember

The sons and daughters
Of sons and daughters

Souls beyond names now
Locals to this day

from **Beyond Basilicas**

Weeknight in Winter

Our balcony flag slapped
Like sailcloth much of the night

Spluttering so ceaselessly
We could imagine its stars and stripes
Blown off by morning

The trees heaved
Our second story shook
Snow came from east of us

And we supposed this was
What it was like to be alive

In Februarys
When the wind held nothing back
When snow fell at will

When ancestors would batten drafty windows
And blanket themselves
And outsleep howling in the eaves
Splatterings against the glass

Or alone   or in pairs   lie low

Wide-eyed   all ears

As though stowed below decks

In heavy seas

from **Memorial Days**

3

The veterans march to Memorial Park
And mark time
And stand at attention
And under the arching maples go
Silent to honor the dead
Some of them
From the old school on Harford Street

Some from the 58,000 of my generation
Brothers long-gone with their unborn children
Remembered now as the fifty-star flag
Exhales   snaps and sags its shoulders
As   at half-staff   the black and white
Of the still-missing
Lifts once and goes limp

Gone   the running back who enlisted
Gone   Warriors and Saints
Whose numbers came up

Gone   the politician flicking his candy
Gone   the black and white of the first TV's

Gone   replaced with
Less-menacing-looking facilities
The old brick munitions factories

And   dead themselves
Ancient history in fact
To most of those
Assembling around war memorials

Presidents who pled the oath
And misled
And kept our small-town graveyards fed

Gone too   the inventors of the last century
Gone to dust   its engineers   its charioteers

Though on black and white balloon tires
Some of the stunning
Monstrosities they designed
Roll before our eyes
Spit-shined
Hearse-like in the blinding sun

Key to the House

We'd keep it hidden among stones
And for our own use

We'd work the kerfed brass
Into the door at all hours

Now   feeling in darkness
For the right key on a ring full of keys

Fingers may skim the chimney's
Nubbed rubble skin again

Any one of us may come
Tumbling a lock

Standing suddenly stock-still
Listening at the threshold for voices

from **Backstory**

6

And one generation passed
And another one came
And one thing led to another

Before long   we kibitz cordlessly
From our porches and backyards
Rome fiddles with semantics
As the proclivities of certain clergy
Come to light

Blue laws loosen
Speed limits lift as highways gyre out
As throughways sprout their express lanes
As life   the living of it one day to the next
Gets less affordable somehow
Even as incomes couple
Even while offspring diminish

And new fathers   new mothers
Do what they have to do
To hold their own   strapped in many of them
Before the crows caw
Flocking entrance ramps   flying freeways
Braking heavily and funneling down
Saint Christopher velcroed to a dashboard

Rosary dangling from a rear view
Radios cranked   red white and blue
Tattering antennas in the dawn's early light

And we shop
On the old days of rest
Roll dice in the unreal cities

Suddenly phones fold up
And slip into purses and vibrate thighs

Towers collapse

One old pope dies
And another old pope
Pops up in his place

Evangelists insist these are
At long last   the last days

Politicians promise
Statisticians reminisce

A few choose Chekhov
Fewer still Camus

And some are sorry to say
It could be true

That nothing's new under the sun
That things'll get fair
Only in the next life

Yet others
Others on long commutes
Come to see just how
Good news becomes no news at all
How   above the fold
Even in a little hill town paper
News sources lead
With what breeds hopelessness

See how no camera crew
Assembles this spring afternoon
When the yellow bus draws up
Under the wide maples
Their rust-colored buds about to burst

See how many miracles are missed
One after another
As grade school sons and daughters
Step down with their backpacks
Carrying their coats

Vanity of vanities
See how no pollster shows up
To total the souls

Who call out from their steering wheels
For the safekeeping of these least ones

To Yahweh   to the Risen Christ
To Allah   to Vishnu
To the gods of cul-de-sacs
To angels of intersections
And alleys and avenues

Citizen-saints who live in the world
Who go one holy moment to the next
Mostly unnoticed
By the powers and principalities that be
Who do their jobs
Who pray more or less breath by breath
Beyond basilicas
Barely moving their lips

Sunday

Early over the footbridge
Up cemetery hills
Early treading the logging road's steady rise
Out of the self

Stumped   leaf-littered
Peppered with fallen limbs
Its ruts clumped with deer grass
Its verge loose with laurel

Where roses riot in an unfarmed field
A rock fence tumbles in the undergrowth
A clear-cut shimmers with birch

Sunday
And looking out far from this ledge
Above steeples   fire lines   washouts   ravines
With the river stitching like silver thread
Through the valley below

Good
The way daylight bathes
Our miniature town

The way shale paths discontinue
The way spirit awakens in skin
As a breeze lifts scotch pine and cedar

Good
That red bird on a rhododendron
This spring-fed water   pooling   releasing
Sluicing stones of every transgression

Approaching All Souls' Day

Dusk
Standing at the end of the driveway

The man pokes his rake
Into a leaf pile

And   remembering their names
Stirs up smoke

Incense
Flames

Notes

Americans By Turns Pg.2

Knowing our inheritance
Was in truth
Borrowed from our children
A paraphrase of a saying often attributed to
Native Americans and found in Wendell Berry's
essay 'The Unforeseen Wilderness.'

And held by us a while
In trust
For safekeeping.
A reference to Elizabeth Bishop's 'Poem'

And said liberty and justice for all
'The Pledge of Allegiance'

Because the town was ours then
And we were the town's
echoing Robert Frost's 'The Gift Outright'

A nation 'of-by-and-for the people' we could see
from Lincoln's Gettysburg Address 1863

The world's best hope
from Thomas Jefferson's first inaugural address
in 1801

And hope was the thing with feathers
Emily Dickinson 1891

To hope against hope
Romans 4:18 KJV

The Perils of Indifference
The title of a speech given at the White House
by Elie Wiesel in 1999

The day or the hour
Matthew 24:36 KJV

The thief
John 10:10 KJV

To the better angels of our nature
Lincoln's first inaugural address 1861

Who are more to us
And more in our meditations
Than you might suppose
Walt Whitman 'Crossing Brooklyn Ferry'

Reverencing a town's
Old bluestone fountain
Located on the northeast corner of Broad and
East High Street, and installed in 1911 by
the Village Improvement Association (VIA) to
provide drinking water for horses in the front,
pedestrians in the back, dogs on either side.

Keeping the republic
Benjamin Franklin 1787 'A republic, if you can
keep it.'

First Names Pg.18

'That summer . . .' 1793. Philadelphia, a city of 50,000 and the temporary capital of the United States, was ravaged by a yellow fever epidemic. Thousands died. More than 20,000 fled, among them John Biddis, who made his way 130 miles north to lands he purchased along the Delaware River, which in 1796 he named Milford.

The Borough Pg.20

'I arrive today . . .' echoes an early Irish prayer called The Deer's Cry (also known as St. Patrick's Breastplate), which begins: 'I arise today.'

Looking Out Pg.24

Tom Hoff, a founder of The Historic Preservation Trust of Pike County, instrumental in establishing Milford's Historic Districts.

Dick Snyder, philanthropist, preservationist, a founder of the Milford Enhancement Committee and the Greater Pike Community Foundation.

The Corner Pg.28

East High Street Looking West Across Broad Street
Late 19th Century

Governor Gifford Pinchot
Speaking at the Dedication of the Soldiers and Sailors
Memorial July 4th, 1931
Upwards of 2,000 people were in attendance

Miserere Pg.40
Miserere: Latin. 'Be Merciful.'

God's Acre Pg.49
God's Acre: an early term for a cemetery.

Remembrance Place Park (sometimes called The
Old Dimmick Cemetery) is located in Milford
Borough at the corner of West Ann Street and
Elderberry Alley.

Acknowledgments

Thank you Eamon Grennan — friend, master-painter with the language — for those walks through the landscape and architecture of the Vassar campus, all the while catching up, sharing news about our families, our daily work, the world . . . For that morning we ducked into the archives to read through Elizabeth Bishop's manuscripts: what a gift to witness her great poems taking shape. I'm ever grateful for the tea and the time we spent reviewing my latest 'batch.'

Thank you Bill Kiger (1942-2026) — Friend for many years, friend of poetry, citizen-by-example, who asked me to read some of the poems in this collection at The Historic Preservation Trust's annual awards ceremonies.

The Columns Museum for help in researching the Soldiers and Sailors Memorial, its history and dedication.

The American Legion Post 139, Milford, Pennsylvania, and members of the veterans organizations who approved my reading of 'The Corner' on Memorial Day, 2017.

Thanks to local publications that saw fit to publish poems in this book: *The Journal, Pike County Dispatch, Pike County Courier.*

Remembering

Charles and Cecelia O'Neil

Tommy O'Neil

Stephen Fuqua, III

Tim Fuqua

Mary Ann Fuqua

Stephen O. and Frances Fuqua

About The Author

Chuck O'Neil has written six poetry collections, most recently **Americans By Turns**. He lives in Milford, Pennsylvania, where he and his wife, Celeste, have lived since 1982. They have four children and three grandchildren. In 2022 he was named Poet Laureate of Milford.

Photo by Marie Liu

www.chuckoneilauthor.com

www.ingramcontent.com/pod-product-compliance
Lightning Source LLC
Chambersburg PA
CBHW021341060726
47591CB00006B/2128